THE HOOPOE'S CROWN

THE HOOPOE'S CROWN

POEMS BY
JACQUELINE OSHEROW

AMERICAN POETS CONTINUUM SERIES, NO. 96

BOA Editions, Ltd. ❋ *Rochester, NY* ❋ *2005*

First Edition
05 06 07 08 7 6 5 4 3 2 1

Publications by BOA Editions, Ltd.—
a not-for-profit corporation under section 501 (c) (3)
of the United States Internal Revenue Code—
are made possible with the assistance of grants from
the Literature Program of the New York State Council on the Arts;
the Literature Program of the National Endowment for the Arts;
the Sonia Raiziss Giop Charitable Foundation; the Lannan Foundation;
the Mary S. Mulligan Charitable Trust; the County of Monroe, NY;
the Rochester Area Community Foundation;
the Elizabeth F. Cheney Foundation; the Ames-Amzalak Memorial Trust
in memory of Henry Ames, Semon Amzalak and Dan Amzalak;
the Chadwick-Loher Foundation in honor of Charles Simic and Ray Gonzalez;
the Steeple-Jack Fund; the Chesonis Family Foundation,
as well as contributions from many individuals nationwide.

See Colophon on page 104 for special individual acknowledgments.

Cover Design: Lisa Mauro
Cover Art: Ketubbah, Kouilvattam, 1909, courtesy of the Israel Museum, Jerusalem/
    Nahum Slapak
Interior Design and Composition: Richard Foerster
Manufacturing: McNaughton & Gunn, Lithographers
BOA Logo: Mirko

Library of Congress Cataloging-in-Publication Data

Osherow, Jacqueline.
  The hoopoe's crown : poems / by Jacqueline Osherow.— 1st ed.
    p. cm.—(American poets continuum series ; v. 96)
  ISBN 1–929918–72–0 (trade pbk. : alk. paper)
  I. Title. II. Series.

  PS3565.S545H66 2005
  811'.54—dc22

2005017457

BOA Editions, Ltd.
Thom Ward, Editor
David Oliveiri, Chair
A. Poulin, Jr., President & Founder (1938–1996)
260 East Avenue, Rochester, NY 14604
www.boaeditions.org

The Hoopoe's Crown

Contents

IV

I

My Version: Medieval Acrostic

Jealousy? Homage? Longing? Superstition?
All I know is, I want to join those guys
Calling God's name, writing their own
Quietly, in steady pieces, as if praise
Unmasks the giver as it goes along,
Existing and singing simultaneous.
Let me in, guys—even if I'm wrong;
I'm not fit for unremitting chaos.
Nudge me when another cornered word
Escapes as firmament the moment it's uttered.

Eccentric Fractals: Isaiah, Math, and Snow

A swift, thick snow, its whiteness so complete
I think I'm in Isaiah's fulfilled promise.
Remember? *For behold I create*

new heavens and a new earth—but he's precise
and these are, after all, the same old heavens,
the same old earth, even an old disguise:

white sheets across chairs, tables, beds, divans.
The universe in linens . . . so why am I
doing a geometric proof without the givens?

For example: which is earth and which is sky?
And what, precisely, does Isaiah mean?
It's not as if we'll have the chance to try,

even superficially, to fathom this version—
the earth alone, much less what's beyond.
We haven't got sufficient information.

But I'd love to watch the heavens and earth abscond
(I see them arm in arm, like that illustration
of Mother Goose's fleeing dish and spoon). Planned

obsolescence? Or just a brief vacation?
And where would we be? Would our feet touch ground
or some wholly other substance? Ocean not ocean?

Air not air? What would carry sound?
Unless Isaiah's speaking of our own perception,
how the earth and heavens always come around,

eventually, to our own lines of vision,
which means, I guess, it's just ourselves we see.
Can we never let anything objective in?

I suspect—too late—there's unexpected beauty
in a wholly different kind of orientation;
I was trying to help my daughter with geometry

And there it was: the perfect explanation
of the world the way it is: *similarity*—
fractals, tiny bursts of correlation

in everything: a vein, a leaf, a tree.
We just have to find the right way in,
which is where that austere branch of poetry—

algebra—might offer some instruction:
at once precise and full of mystery
with its abiding metaphor—x or n—

a universe of absolute affinity
but variable—that's us, the variable.
Though there are fixed anomalies, like   ,

that master poet who can simply eyeball
a flawless circle every single time.
What a slob she is, utterly unmanageable,

always something out of place, never a modicum
of self-restraint or order, endless excess,
but those circles of hers: each one sublime.

She's my role model! Maybe I'm not hopeless!
Maybe there's even the minutest chance
that my own array of bafflement and mess

could actually get *out upon circumference.*
The closest I've come is this white on white—
if only I could conjure up some eloquence

I haven't borrowed, some perfect insight,
something to which x and n have access:
x being   's airtight final digit,

n, the way a whirlwind begets ice.
Or call *x* the ratio of life to art
and *n* what muses, left alone, discuss.

x is that open problem, my husband's heart.
(What axiom applies? Will it ever show?)
Okay, it isn't poetry, but it's a start

since *x* and *n* are what I need to know.
x is a black hole's extreme interior,
n is what's underlying all this snow,

itself an intimation of the white frontier
x milliseconds past the speed of light
where *x* and *n*, as thought and sound, cohere.

x is ambiguous; *x* is concrete;
x is the chanting underneath each rhyme;
on the other hand, *x* makes rhymes obsolete.

Do I really mean that? What a shame.
Isn't *x* any bull's-eye you can fling?
The absolute and infinite delirium

of whatever captures *n* and makes it sing?
Isaiah, for example, listen to him.
Unless you think that talking to God is cheating.

I say: whatever sharpens your aim. . . .
Think of those gorgeous circles of Isaiah's—
how, led by him, even the humblest item

can navigate a host of unguessed likenesses,
then relocate itself, wholly transformed.
You don't believe me? I have witnesses:

the heavens and earth (the old ones) strong-armed
to listen and give ear in his very first line.
I'm sure—prophecy's persuasive—they conformed.

Then he betrayed them with his long-term plan
to do away with them. Were they bad listeners?
They can't have been as inattentive as I've been.

Snow—I chant it yearly—is a refuge for sinners
in Isaiah (chapter one, verse seventeen).
I'm just one of his scarlet petitioners

inspired by this blizzard to come clean.
Come, let us reason together, he implores us,
his voice solicitous suddenly, so serene

I almost think he hates being censorious
and regrets what he's just made us undergo.
That's when we get the unforgettable, glorious

business about scarlet sins and snow.
I don't know about you, but I'm persuaded.
Who says you can't divide a number by zero?

The most exquisite truths are all occluded
like the heavens and the earth in all this snow,
each ornate, six-sided speck encoded

with everything I've ever wanted to know,
a fractal of a fractal of a fractal
of that primary, still burning fleck of snow

touched to Isaiah's lips by that angel.
Isaiah had only seen snow from a distance
and so mistook it for a burning coal.

I've been let in on this truth by chance—
just now, this blizzard. See? My lips still burn
from a random flake that tried to make an entrance.

Was a seraph here with tongs? Will he return?
I will put my words in your mouth (How did I miss this?
Too much writing, too little reading. When will I learn?)

that I may plant the heavens—is that a promise?—
and lay the foundations of the earth. Words
in *our* mouths, this time, not like Genesis.

But there's a catch: we have to beat our swords
into ploughshares first. Feed the hungry.
And oversee all kinds of farfetched concords:

leopard/lamb, wolf/calf, asp/baby.
Do what you like, but I won't hold my breath.
Is it blasphemy to deem Isaiah's prophecy,

at times, almost as slippery as my math?
I, too, meant to be precise, to equal something,
but I had to give my x and n some breadth

if they were going to have a chance to sing.
Isaiah, too, seems familiar with this problem.
Of course, he had a real gift for believing,

not to mention a coherent social program.
But, still, he's mostly after what's abstruse:
inaccessibility's compulsive beauty. Come,

let's reason together. What do we have to lose?
Who says we can't impersonate this snow?
Quick, before it all starts to diffuse.

Multiply x by n. Divide by zero.
Make the universe an offer it can't refuse.
Then read Isaiah aloud. Pretend it's true.

Think *waters of salvation.* Think *watchman's voice.*
Think *as one whom his mother comforts I'll comfort you.* . . .
Your heart will rejoice, your bones will flourish like the grass. . . .
Behold I'll make the earth and heavens new.

Desert Postcards

1. Highway Ninety: the Aravah

> *Thus saith the Lord: they found grace in the desert,*
> *the people left over by the sword.*
> —Jeremiah 31:2

I should have
known this,
should have
been able
to imagine
how the rock's
austerity consoles
itself, unrolling
its elaborate
double scroll,
to flood its
pale expanse
with sacred
words, those

fragments in
the ancient jars
redundant, since
all the rock
around the
Qumran Caves
was already thick
with those
same words.

Even from
a moving
car, you can

see them:
their burning
columns in strict,
efficient rows,
like tiny
nimble caravans
across the desert.
See how they
come as close
as language comes
to the indivisibility
of prime numbers?
Prime words, then,
perfect words.

You'll say they're
in my head,
and so they are.

But they're also
out there, rising
off the rock,
what Jeremiah
meant by *grace*
in the desert:
how this
emptiness
redeems itself
with words.

And my three
beauties, dreaming
in the back
are *the nation*
left over by
the sword, or,
rather, in their
case, their

grandparents'
case, the rifle
butt, typhus,
the crematoria,

their existence
inexplicable,
except by
miracle—
unless you
prefer to
call it
prophecy:
thus saith the Lord.

2. Eyn Avdat

You've stumbled
on the unremitting
aftermath of
earthly argument
with outer space,
the vast, empty
empire still
victorious, holding
forth at this,
its farthest
outpost: a stark,
completely
barren curve
of cliffs,
one meteorite's
urgent last request.

Here, if you enter
through a crevice
in the rock,

you come upon
two sapphire pools
so motionless,
they double
as a breeding
ground for earth
and sky, their
cool, dark
origins beneath
the depths
of rock, in God's
holy language
called an *eye*

as if water
in such a place
required vision—
no celestial
body, but a voice
in a whirl-
wind, revealing
the marauding wings
of mother eagles,
their ravenous
fledglings defenseless
in these cliffs, high
above the womb
that begat ice.

3. Judean Hills

Here, you can rest
with open eyes,
this futile coupling
of rock and air
at least incapable
of accusation,

devoid as it is
of even a skeletal
acacia, where a stray
parched animal
might scrounge
some shade,

as if to disclose
to my ungenerous
heart that it's not
the world's only
source of harshness

and I'm so grateful
for this, grateful
for emptiness,
and that my whole
botched universe
is out of sight

that I'm even willing
to call this beautiful,
to wait for nightfall
and the extravagant
tales of stars.

Rest yourself, rest,
murmurs the empty-handed
horizon. . . . Jacob
fell asleep not far
from here . . . and he'd
committed far worse
crimes than yours.

Fata Morgana

The righteous shall flourish like the date palm . . .
—Psalm 92:13

There I was at the literal
depths of the earth: nothing
but rock, saltwater, salt, parched air
and a redundant sign with an arrow
reading *S'dom*, as if there were another
possible explanation. I wanted to see

for myself what a woman looks like
who has watched God wreak vengeance
on her home, but there wasn't a single
pillar of salt anywhere. I would have thought
there'd be a host of them—in such
dry air the tears evaporate so quickly—
perhaps we should have tried a different road?

But then we got distracted by a shock
of green: row after row after row
of righteous palms, their fronds
pressed against the blistering air
to offer anyone who passed a gift of shade

and a fleeting glimpse
of the colossal move
from a bleak, closefisted
stretch of wilderness

to a land flowing with milk
and so much honey
that an iridescent flock of emerald bee eaters
had flown all the way from inmost Africa
to gorge themselves on swarms of promised bees.

I saw them with my own eyes: green on green,
their unreal wings (studs of sapphire, shafts of gold)
almost invisible against the blinding leaves
that had sworn off any dew or mist or rain—
sustained by a cool unearthly earthly secret.

Lot's wife was foolish to look back,
when she might have seen this in front of her,
except that sometimes
it isn't beauty we're after
but an even more ethereal apparition

that finds its double in our memory
and lets us know when something is our own—

usually a reassuring notion
though it can cause—especially
around there—so much trouble

and this woman hadn't thought
to bring her name with her,
much less her hand mirror, her emerald earrings . . .
and even if she had been self-possessed
when her husband said they weren't coming back

she couldn't have brought along
the perfectly positioned tent flap
through which she'd watched
her mountains at their rose toilette
transform themselves each night
to deep vermilion, their sighs
a makeshift trove of evening breeze.

Anyway, as I told you, I forgot her
in a momentary trance of brilliant green
on which I, too, am frantic to make a claim

and—though I don't mean anything
explicitly political—I know this
entangles me in bitter chaos,
hatred, terror, torture, war.

Is it worth it, just so I can write:
My bee eaters, My date palms,
My dazzling mirage of desert green?
I, who could sit anywhere, write almost anything?

The truth is I didn't realize what I was doing.
I just took a simple backward glimpse
and there, in front of me, corporeal
was something I'd thought only lived in words,
inviolable—a holy language—
words you couldn't even paraphrase,
much less have three-dimensional before your eyes.

I dispensed with them as soon as I had the chance,
dispensed, in fact, with half the famous promise,
didn't even look for any sign of milk
in my delirium at all that honey,

which I identified,
it turns out, thoroughly by accident.
Biblical honey required no bees
but came from dates—another
gift of selfless palms—

and, therefore, had nothing to do
with my enchanted bee eaters,
first sighted in the area in the fifties,
all those idealists making the desert bloom
naturally enough attracting bees
and then, after a while, their gorgeous predators

but still, it's too late, I've glimpsed
my vision—I can't dissociate

God's ancient balmy promise
from the gemstones beating
in those bright, green wings,

which amounts, like it or not, to a kind of claim,
not that I'm in favor of displaced people,
retribution, ethnic hatred, misery,

but a person—even a poet—every once in a while
needs to know that words are linked to things

even if it means looking out
on insurmountable earthly complications,
the messes so intrinsic
that God Himself
has only tried to solve them with destruction.

(Maybe it was His own incompetence
He so didn't want Lot's wife to see.)

I was squeamish—for years
I wanted no part of this—

and I'm not sure I know what happened next;
there I was, my head turned back, my eyes opened:
I just wanted to see it before it exploded
or maybe I *was* curious about my home;
everybody has to come from somewhere

and Philadelphia, though among
the more generous way stations
in the course of all that drawn-out wandering,
is far too haphazard for consideration.

So now, with no warning,
I'm suddenly stuck
in this place of warring claims
and endless trouble,

with all these people crowded
onto a single sliver of vision
murmuring to themselves *my land, my home.*

I can't even see the oasis from here
just the Dead Sea and endless desert.
Nothing lives here. Not even sound
except for snatches of oldies on Radio Jordan
(clearer than any Israeli station)
dispensed by the occasional passing car

and the intermittent rumbling
of artillery in the distance—practice
maneuvers at an outlying base—
like stifled, systematic thunder.

Even durable words come up empty.
Righteousness, for example,
is a good deal easier
for a date palm
than for a human being.

For one thing: what honey do I have to offer?
Here, there's only salt and bitterness

and as for shade, I wouldn't get between
even the most brutal sun and anything;
I can't help it. I need light. I want to see:
the thin layer of salt
over the bleached-out rock
in this godforsaken outpost
of the wilderness

or its lush, inexplicable
antithesis, just down
the road, outside my
line of vision, tangled

up in outstretched fronds
and wings, baffling
the promised air with green.

Egrets in Be'er Sheva

What language is it
in which egret feathers
mean purity? In which—
my friend swears it—
Isaiah's scarlet sins
go white as egret
feathers, not as snow?
Isaiah could so easily
have mentioned egrets—
I saw them in Be'er Sheva,
crowding out the trees,
each slender, graceful
torso white as snow,
so many I thought
the trees would
topple over. Though
it was summer, they
seemed to have no
leaves, just slender,
graceful arcs of blameless
snow, which made,
I have to admit,
an absolute racket.
But, surely, it was
that ecstatic noise
that got me—for
once—to lift my eyes,
the very sound Isaiah's
voice was after:
though your sins be
scarlet, they shall be
white as the egrets
in these trees, but then
he was afraid he'd

divulged his secret:
his immaculate source
wasn't God at all, but
fleet, white arrows
slashing the heavens,
divvying the clouds
among the startled trees,
snow-white feathers
flying as they'd go.
He crossed out "egret"
and wrote "snow."

The Stork in the Heaven

Yea, the stork in the heaven knoweth her appointed times.

—Jeremiah 8:7

I first saw them at the walled city
of Avila, the German woman beside me
utterly ecstatic: *It has been my dream
to see storks flying above the walls
of Avila.* Could those really be storks?
Those leggy buffoons had this much grace?

Not that I'd question any source of grace,
especially combined with such a wing capacity.
I finally understood about the fabled storks:
I'd love to think such creatures had brought *me*,
set me down softly on some gold, medieval walls
and left me on my own to wake and dream.

And they did bring off a miracle: a realized dream!
What had my woman done to deserve such grace?
Though,who knows? Maybe storks on Avila's walls
are as rare as pigeons in New York City.
Does it matter? They're the stuff of dreams to me
though I can't say I thought much about those storks

till last spring in the Galilee (Africa's storks'
layover to Europe) when the woman and her dream
returned: a stork flew directly over me,
all beak, forward motion and utter grace.
We were near Afulah, an ugly city,
good falafel, but no medieval walls—

just as well, since, in those parts, city walls
are embedded with shards of glass. Alighting storks
would be injured, like the birds in the Holy City,

casualties in the longtime war of dream.
You'd have thought (you'd have been wrong) that God's grace
doesn't require backup from an army.

But the truth is I was glad to see that army
in Jerusalem with my kids, climbing those walls.
That's where we saw the glass. (No sign of grace.)
But how did I get here? Wasn't I talking about storks,
my German woman, her captured dream
and not that battleground, the Holy City?

Why must I always talk atrocity?
Who said anything about an army?
This is a poem about dream.
Let's leave behind Avila's exquisite walls;
they're not the only summer home of storks.
I've yet to tell my own tale of grace.

But still, there's background material: *they found grace
in the desert, the people left over by the sword.* Historicity.
(Don't worry. I'm getting back to storks.)
The way we wandered, dodging local priest and army
and probably hit Avila, before more Eastern ghetto walls
crammed us in, with parchment, ink and dream.

Say what you like about us. We can dream
and we can also, I've seen it, locate grace
without—you'll forgive me—the shard-embedded walls
of a scarred, salted, wrangled-over city.
In fact, every year, as the breeze grew balmy
we did it beneath chimneyfuls of storks.

I have it on authority. For us, storks
are the stuff of summer chimneys, not of dream.
It's true. My cousin Beka told me.
(I was visiting Chicago, where she'd landed by the grace
of God—via Gura Mura, Trasnistria, Tel Aviv, Panama City—
first horrors, then miracles, renewals.)

She'd hear them stirring through her bedroom walls.
Nesting in her chimney: two great storks
(this was before the Nazis overran her little city
when she still had the luxury of dream . . .)
charmed her with their unexpected grace,
their outspread wings' impulsive alchemy.

I can't explain why this should mean so much to me.
Surely, my grandma, through her childhood's walls,
would also awaken to this stroke of grace:
all the way from Africa, two storks.
Perhaps it was of them she used to dream
at her machine in her sweatshop in her new, shrill city:

storks gracing the preposterous walls
of the newly dreamed-up skyscrapers of New York City
and dangling from their beaks: the likes of me.

Autumn Psalm

A full year passed (the seasons keep me honest)
since I last noticed this same commotion.
Who knew God was an abstract expressionist?

I'm asking myself—the very question
I asked last year, staring out at this array
of racing colors, then set in motion

by the chance invasion of a Steller's jay.
Is *this* what people mean by *speed of light*?
My usually levelheaded mulberry tree

hurling arrows everywhere in sight—
its bow: the out-of-control Virginia creeper
my friends say I should do something about,

whose vermilion went at least a full shade deeper
at the provocation of the upstart blue,
the leaves (half green, half gold) suddenly hyper

in savage competition with that red and blue—
tohubohu returned, in living color.
Kandinsky: where were you when I needed you?

My attempted poem would lie fallow a year;
I was so busy focusing on the desert's
stinginess with everything but rumor.

No place even for the spectrum's introverts—
rose, olive, gray—no pigment at all—
and certainly no room for shameless braggarts

like the ones that barge in here every fall
and make me feel like an unredeemed failure
even more emphatically than usual.

And here they are again, their fleet allure
still more urgent this time—the desert's gone;
I'm through with it, want something fuller—

why shouldn't a person have a little fun,
some utterly unnecessary extravagance?
Which was—at least I think it was—God's plan

when He set up (such things are never left to chance)
that one split-second assignation
with genuine, no-kidding-around omnipotence—

what, for lack of better words, I'm calling *vision*.
You breathe in, and, for once, there's something there.
Just when you thought you'd learned some resignation,

there's real resistance in the nearby air
until the entire universe is swayed.
Even that desert of yours isn't quite so bare

and God's not nonexistent; He's just been waylaid
by a host of what no one could've foreseen.
He's got plans for you: this red-gold-green parade

is actually a fairly detailed outline.
David never needed one, but he's long dead
and God could use a little recognition.

He promises. It won't go to His head
and if you praise Him properly (an autumn psalm!
Why didn't *I* think of that?) you'll have it made.

But while it's true that my Virginia creeper praises Him,
its palms and fingers crimson with applause,
that the local breeze is weaving Him a diadem,

inspecting my tree's uncut gold for flaws,
I came to talk about the way that violet-blue
sprang the greens and reds and yellows

into action: actual motion. I swear it's true
though I'm not sure I ever took it in.
Now I'd be prepared, if some magician flew

into my field of vision, to realign
that dazzle out my window yet again.
It's not likely, but I'm keeping my eyes open

though I still wouldn't be able to explain
precisely what happened to these vines, these trees.
It isn't available in my tradition.

For this, I would have to be Chinese,
Wang Wei, to be precise, on a mountain,
autumn rain converging on the trees,

a cassia flower nearby, a cloud, a pine,
washerwomen heading home for the day,
my senses and the mountain so entirely in tune

that when my stroke of blue arrives, I'm ready.
Though there is no rain here: the air's shot through
with gold on golden leaves. Wang Wei's so giddy

he's calling back the dead: *Li Bai! Du Fu!*
Guys! You've got to see this—autumn sun!
They're suddenly hell-bent on learning Hebrew

in order to get inside the celebration,
which explains how they wound up where they are
in my university library's squashed domain.

Poor guys, it was Hebrew they were looking for,
but they ended up across the aisle from Yiddish—
some Library of Congress cataloger's sense of humor:

the world's calmest characters and its most skittish
squinting at each other, head to head,
all silently intoning some version of kaddish

for their nonexistent readers, one side's dead
(the twentieth century's lasting contribution)
and the other's insufficiently learned

to understand a fraction of what they mean.
The writings in the world's most spoken language
across from one that can barely get a minyan.

Sick of *lanzmen,* the *yidden* are trying to engage
the guys across the aisle in some conversation:
How, for example, do you squeeze an image

into so few words, respectfully asks Glatstein.
Wang Wei, at first, doesn't understand the problem
but then he shrugs his shoulders, mumbles *Zen*

. . . but, please, I, myself, overheard a poem,
in the autumn rain, once, on a mountain.
How do you do it? I believe it's called a psalm?

Glatstein's cronies all crack up in unison.
Okay, groise macher, give him an answer.
But Glatstein dons his yarmulke (who knew he had one?)

and starts the introduction to the morning prayer,
Pisukei di zimrah, psalm by psalm.
Wang Wei is spellbound, the stacks' stale air

suddenly a veritable balm
and I'm so touched by these amazing goings-on
that I've forgotten all about the autumn

staring straight at me: still alive, still golden.
What's gold, anyway, compared to poetry?
a trick of chlorophyll, a trick of sun.

True. It was something, my changing tree
with its perfect complement: a crimson vine,
both thrown into panic by a Steller's jay,

but it's hard to shake the habit of digression.
Wandering has always been my people's way
whether we're in a desert or narration.

It's too late to emulate Wang Wei
and his solitary years on that one mountain
though I'd love to say what I set out to say

just once. Next autumn, maybe. *What's the occasion?*
Glatstein will shout over to me from the bookcase
(that is, if he's paying any attention)

and, finally, I'll look him in the face.
Quick. Out the window, Yankev. It's here again.

II

Ri'e Yazmin

Who will ascend the mountain of God
and who will stand in His Holy place?
Those with clean palms and pure of heart.
—Psalm 24

Ri'e yazmin . . .
—Shmuel HaNagid

*Córdoba,
Lejana y sola.*

*Jaca negra, luna grande,
y aceitunas en mi alforja.
Aunque sepa los caminos
yo nunca llegaré a Córdoba*
—Federico García Lorca

Madinat al-Zahra—wasn't that the name
of my jasmine ruin, my source of jasmine
when, trailing Lorca and the Sephardim,

I'd gone to feast my eyes on Southern Spain?
I was ogling *Córdoba, lejana y sola:*
its fleets of low white buildings shot with sun,

the mosque disfigured by a Christian cupola,
the synagogue intact, complete with psalms—
but there were rumors from *Alf Laylah Walaylah*

of red-gold stags and falcons dripping gems,
floors, whose leaf motifs, coral and ivory,
embraced tenacious lapis pentagrams.

Surely I had to splurge for a taxi?
When would I ever be that close again?
(I never dreamed a book of Hebrew poetry—

Shmuel HaNagid, a new translation—
would offer me its name from the introduction.)
When I got there, it was completely overgrown.

I suppose that's how I came upon that jasmine—
my first jasmine—growing wild
on a hillside where a palace should have been;

my *Blue Guide*'s promises were not fulfilled.
There were olive trees, grasses to my thigh,
a couple of marble columns, but no gold,

no walls inlaid with ivory, jasper, ebony.
I'd read too fast; that lush description
was only of long vanished luxury:

the golden bestiary—where each pearl or jewel
defining every eye or feather or mane
would repeat itself in droplets as they rose and fell

around the central courtyard's massive fountain—
had long been ravaged, with its fountain's marble
(chiseled in Damascus, ocean-green).

Nothing at all was left of the reception hall
for foreign envoys, whose affairs of state
dissolved into the quicksilver reflecting pool

that shattered any passing glint of light
into a billion feats of incandescence.
The one vestige of the dense, elaborate

daily apparatus of magnificence
(a hundred loaves a day just for the fish
in ornamental ponds) was a fragrance,

an intoxicating fragrance, subtle *and* lavish,
at least to this itinerant self-deceiver,
thrilled when her own flawed world would vanish

in the face of any rickety leftover
from some lost—hence inexhaustible—domain.
I was always a born shill, a believer;

I sank my face in what I guessed was jasmine
and the razed city-palace of Caliph Rahman
became—unconditionally—mine,

is mine whenever I chance on jasmine:
the dreamed al-Zahra—not what I saw:
those jeweled kestrels splashing in a fountain

replaced, in Agrigento, the Temple of Hera
and in Petra, after hours of dreaming stone,
I briefly stepped down at Madinat al-Zahra

from an amethyst and ivory palanquin:
five modest petals, tear-shaped, white,
their meeting place a pale incarnadine

whose poison turns each petal fatal violet
until a purple blossom falls away.
The great Shmuel HaNagid compares it

in *Look at the Jasmine* to a *pallid boy*
with the blood of men with clean palms in his palm
in the very book of Hebrew poetry

where I found al-Zahra's long-unthought-of name.
My newfound poet had also been there—
at the moment when the palace was in its prime—

and still he chose to write about my flower.
Maybe the very same one. Do plants endure?
The poem barely did. It was lost forever,

until Chaim Bialik, on a fund-raising tour
for modern Hebrew publishing—a crackpot scheme—
was offered what he called *an incomparable treasure*

in his brand-new Hebrew in a letter home:
a Yiddish-turned-Hebrew poet—try to imagine—
devouring poems lost for a millennium

in a language that had just become his own.
His and not his; mine and not mine
since what do we know of a gazelle, a fawn,

or how it might feel to be an older man
dazzled by a young boy in the moonlight.
The poet's son called it *love of the divine*

and did not censor his father poet
when he collected the poems for the *Diwan*.
Still, we get a glimpse of how the moonlight

erased the stars, the boy erased the moon,
abetted by bits of psalms and Jeremiah
inlaid in his poems like the inlaid stone

of the chamber walls of Madinat al-Zahra . . .
which rose up from the foothills five miles west
of Shmuel HaNagid's native Córdoba—

a little over an hour's walk, if you walk fast . . .
but the dates don't exactly coincide—
HaNagid and al-Zahra *did* coexist—

but he ruled from the Alhambra. HaNagid—
I checked the dates again—was only twenty
when the city was captured, his family fled

and the Berbers immortalized their sovereignty
by razing the great al-Zahra to the ground.
I'd thought he lived at al-Zahra, with such certainty—

but I just can't keep the facts straight in my mind
in the face of all this dizzying description.
Al-Zahra's name is only mentioned as background

in my book's long historical introduction—
HaNagid became vizier to Caliph Rahman,
grandson of the great al-Zahra Rahman,

the one who lined the route from Northern Spain
with two ranks of soldiers, whose angled, upraised swords
made a solid sweeping canopy against the sun.

Now all that's left of them is words.
A chance mention. Historical background.
The pearl-encrusted animals and courtyards

absolutely nowhere to be found.
But maybe that destruction was HaNagid's muse.
He wanted his world to go on, spellbound,

mimicked quicksilver with a light-struck phrase
and then another . . . call it lyric barrage.
He did, apparently, have that kind of hubris:

named himself the David of his age
and perhaps he was—we'll never know
about the other poets of his vintage,

whose poems weren't copied in Aleppo,
kept for hundreds of years, brought to London.
How can we be certain that there were no

other poets sizing up the moon
in Andalusian gardens, in illicit love?
Perhaps they never bothered to write down

the choruses of voices they were dreaming of,
who also murmured, meaning it, *look! jasmine*
or perhaps they simply couldn't bear to leave—

despite the burning—a native town;
maybe they never learned to read or write;
it's not, after all, as if no woman

had ever taken in the canceled moonlight
from an elongated window in the chamber
where she amazed her handmaids every night.

There might have been Hebrew poets without number,
Shmuel HaNagid the weakest of them all,
just as his adopted city's Alhambra—

compared to the lost al-Zahra—seemed cramped, small,
its majesty a trifle parsimonious,
no capacity whatever to enthrall.

The Alhambra: my apotheosis
of opulence, excess: pure elation.
I went three times (in between, to Lorca's house:

a bus ride up a hill. No plaque. No sign.
A woman answered, but wouldn't let me in),
each courtyard a bedazzling revelation.

So why, now, should I feel let down
that HaNagid didn't rule from my lost paradise
and why is just the lost palace mine?

and Shmuel HaNagid's—or it could be his
if I decide I'm going to let him in. . . .
It's easy: with fourteen thousand in the palace,

how could he not have known a single one?
He must have been invited at least once
in twenty years. Who knows? Some older man,

some friend, some lover, some chance acquaintance
and, if all else fails, there's always jasmine.
Still, there are limits to extravagance

in even the greediest imagination.
Let's face it, my al-Zahra would be bodiless
without the vast Alhambra to fill it in

and it's so unsettling, this randomness,
how we're victims of what happens to remain.
But, on the other hand, what would change for us

if Madinat al-Zahra hadn't burned down?
Let's say a few choice bits had been preserved,
that some industrious, forward-thinking person

had sifted through the ruins, that she'd saved
a couple of remnants for us from its past?
It's not as if anything has ever been proved.

Well, yes, once. And it almost didn't last:
a man in a garden: *look! jasmine*
he pointed, insisted, cooed, coaxed, confessed

to a woman who routinely used a flying machine,
whose finger could illuminate a house
or spread his poems on a light-struck screen

from which, in an hour or so, she could have access
to more knowledge than he'd ever dreamed
in a quite long lifetime of rare thoughtfulness—

all this in a language not yet tamed
at the moment when he might have listened in,
her entire verbal universe as yet unclaimed

and she, whose voice could carry across an ocean,
who could picture—intact and simultaneous—
both his city palace and its ruin,

could at the same time catch his ear, whisper *yes.*
I see it precisely, your sprig of jasmine,
in which we each, poets both, once thrust a face.

I insist on it. The self-same one,
which flourished on that hillside for a thousand years,
through Caliphs, Berbers, an Inquisition,

the exchange of gutturals for rolling r's,
a blaze of anarchists, drowned out by fascists,
its blossoms fleeting mimics of the stars

that also presided over both our visits
to *Córdoba, far off and alone.*
You realize, Shmuel, we weren't the only poets

to smell that particular sprig of jasmine.
Black workhorse, giant moon
Another was a lot like you: an Andalusian

who also wanted men—wanted them *green*—
only he could never have made out your poems
and I—God's goodness *is* eternal—can.

It's our shared inheritance: changeless columns
full of a strict decorum to observe.
I, too, would've called my poems *Son of Psalms*

or *Daughter*, rather, if I'd had the nerve.
But Lorca's had my heart since high-school Spanish class;
I love a poem with a lunar curve

whose words have never occupied a single place
where my mind or tongue have ever been:
lejana, for example, *aceitunas*

and my momentary favorite: *yazmin.*
(*I'll* never arrive, although I know the roads
and my heart is fairly pure, my white palms clean.)

Each unfamiliar syllable explodes
like lightning in a blizzard in the dead of night
piercing through the whiteness with its blades;

you wake up in an unreal flash of violet-white
and what can you say, but *look! jasmine*
as you watch the snow take on the purple light.

Look! jasmine—and a green marble fountain,
quicksilver, birds of jewel-encrusted gold
and only this instant do I get the pun

(would it even work in thousand-year-old
Hebrew?) *Ri'i yazmin.* Jasmine mirror.
And it's as if a drop of quicksilver had spilled

from the pool onto the vellum, only purer
and even more adept at catching light,
in itself more incisive, brighter, clearer,

and far more frantic to illuminate
than that indecisive trickle from the sun.
Sometimes it's violet, sometimes it's white.

That's what I want: to see myself in jasmine,
to capture and refract another light,
for a woman on a not-yet-discovered moon

of an unknown solar system's outer planet
to know instantly precisely what I mean
despite the hundred decades since I've uttered it,

the unimagined places she'll have seen.
She'll have to have been to earth once, on vacation,
and stopped for God knows what eccentric reason—

something she read, probably—in a garden
and in the singsong syllables of her new tongue
(a hybrid language of earthly origin,

its strings of synonyms immensely long,
any number of roots from English and Japanese)
she will have had this vague desire to sing,

which, years later, when she chances on *this*—
it won't even have to be a good translation—
will call up in her such ecstatic rhapsodies.

Laugh if you want, but a poet needs ambition
to keep talking to the dead, the not-yet born,
since no one actually alive will pay attention.

Besides, if a person has to yearn,
she might as well make something of her yearning
and it *is* rapture—the way a poet's words return,

themselves and not themselves, distant *and* burning,
even if it is a kind of self-delusion,
as if there were no vulnerable planet turning

on the self-same axis, in the same confusion.
And I *am* sure of at least one thing:
Shmuel HaNagid and Lorca were in collusion

to make their Córdoba rise up and sing
despite the falangistas, the Berber conquerors,
that the petals of a jasmine as it's blossoming

will, from the proper angle, double as mirrors
even when there is no jasmine in sight.
Maybe my two Andalusian conjurors

need a matchmaker for this one night.
Let these lines be their one-night stand:
HaNagid will wear purple, Lorca, white;

it doesn't have to look as if it's planned.
They'd naturally gravitate to this sprig of jasmine
here, where the city palace used to stand.

Do you think they'd mind if, at first, I listen in?
Why can't it be Lorca canceling out HaNagid's moon?
HaNagid whom Lorca so wants green?

Lorca thinks he's listening to a gypsy tune
in a not quite familiar, archaic jargon.
But what makes all the air around him sweeten?

Where can it come from, this absurd compulsion
to prowl among the ruins? Look! Jasmine.

III

At the Art Nouveau Synagogue, Rue Pavée

Fool that I am, I think I've come for the design
and it is something, to see an Orthodox *shul*
kept so obsessively in line

by a rule as antithetical as style.
The other matrons and I have a splendid view;
from here, on the women's balcony, it's almost beautiful,

though it's also slightly farcical, this Art Nouveau—
so much silly posturing—yet, such aplomb.
Yesterday, at the museum, as I wandered through

each increasingly excessive Nouveau room,
I thought of every preening piece of furniture
as an ordinary household item

playing dress-up. Where does a sofa get such hauteur?
Where, for that matter, does a house of prayer?
—its curves off-center, contrary to nature,

each angle elongated to a flare,
the walls and ceilings far too high and lean,
every pew, table, bookstand, handrail, chair

trimmed with the telltale long-stemmed lily design,
repeated in fixtures, moldings, even the fretwork
I'm peering through (we women mustn't be seen),

though some of the lily light bulbs have gone dark
and the plans could not have allowed that ugly curtain
or the golden lions on the Holy Ark,

not to mention these thick, round-shouldered men
with untrimmed beards and huge broad-brimmed black hats.
The place calls for an entirely different specimen:

tall and thin in peacock-feather waistcoats,
their languid fingers, swathed in pearl-white gloves,
dangling cigarette holders or lorgnettes.

Not one would look at all like he believes
in anything, and certainly not the call
of the—admittedly not very likely—set of narratives

that a few of the men have started to unscroll
on the outsized center table for that purpose.
I doubt they notice lilies on the wall.

From up here, anyway, they seem oblivious
to everything around them but the task at hand:
the opened Torah for one of them to bless,

and then the portion of the week to chant—
so beautifully, I, too, know where I am
though I have no text to follow. This very instant

the angels have come to call on Abraham
which means a long morning of upheaval:
Sarah's cryptic laugh, the end of Sodom,

Hagar in the desert with Ishmael,
each story punctuated by a blessing—
blessing words—my most beloved ritual—

though I can't do it here. Indeed I'm trespassing
as it is: wearing jeans, my head uncovered.
Probably I shouldn't even sing.

It's forbidden for women's voices to be heard;
they're too erotic, apparently (I beg your pardon).
Recently, Barbra Streisand herself was barred

from some Israel thing in Madison Square Garden
though she'd offered to donate her performance.
I usually have no patience for this ancient burden

but how can I explain? It's my inheritance:
a cluster of stars of David on the Paris map
(I *would* have worn a dress, but I came by chance)

marking spots only a few streets up
from my first stop, on the Rue de Sévigné.
And I remembered standing, years ago, on the doorstep

of an Art Nouveau synagogue in the Marais.
It was closed that afternoon. So here I am
(it had to be one of those stars—and today *is* Saturday)

though I already know these stories' outcome
and I certainly hadn't meant to stay.
But in the enlightened synagogue I attend at home

the Torah isn't chanted quite this way.
This man gives each word a subtle emphasis
as if the simplest pronoun might convey

a mystery incomparably precious—
its rise from the parchment on the table
through the silver pointer to his voice

an obligation so inviolable
you'd think he'd have to fast for forty days
if he were to drop a single syllable,

as a person is required to fast who even sees
the dropping of a Torah on the ground.
(Does it count, I've always wondered, if you close your eyes

or, seeing a Torah falling, turn around?
Are the blind absolved? What if it's dark?)
There isn't a punishment for dropped sound,

but the Torah must be read with no mistake.
The reader rereads anything misread
and the entire congregation is obliged to check

lest some holy letter go unsaid;
this man hasn't been corrected once.
One doesn't blunder with the words of God.

It has nothing to do with reward or penance—
the rules are just a labyrinthine metaphor
for perfect and elusive reverence,

which, for this one instant, I can almost hear
as—the blessing's over—the chant continues:
And after these things, what I've been waiting for.

(A chapter I was made, in Hebrew, to memorize;
our teacher read each verse with one dropped word
which we would have to fill in for a quiz.)

So I can hear the words before they're uttered.
I'm calm throughout the tense, well-planned charade:
the kindling wood, the altar, the binding cord,

the knife stretched above the young boy's head,
all an indelible, flamboyant sham.
Abraham knows this, which is why he's said

to Isaac: *God will provide the ram*,
to his servants: *I and the boy will come back*.
Hasn't God already appeared and promised him

a covenant with this very Isaac
and with *his* heirs, numberless as stars?
And here they are, below me, dressed in black,

their promised presence ringing in their ears
and I, skeptic that I am, also a promise.
And these children running up and down the stairs,

living proof that God can be magnanimous,
that I, myself, could even make a claim
on something unearthly and enormous.

Here's God now, reassuring Abraham.
It's not a question of faith at all, but story.
Sometimes, words themselves can offer asylum

and, if victory's endurance, victory—
albeit a little scattered and far-flung.
Whether there's a God or not, He's robed in glory,

by which I mean the supple Hebrew tongue
as it extracts the majesty from each named thing
and orders it to utter a new song.

But what's happening here? What's all this shouting?
It's as if an explosion hit the room:
wild singing to the man who made the blessing.

They're not throwing candy, so he isn't a groom;
all the hooting, *mazel-tov*ing, clapping, cheers
must mean his newborn girl's been given a name—

one more of the numberless as stars.
Being wicked and something of a killjoy,
I think: I'd also cheer a new workhorse,

but I'm a bit unfair. Joy is joy
and here it is below me, as noisy, pure,
as it would be at any *bris* for a new boy.

I'm not even averse to the special prayer
that she grow to Torah, *chupah* and good deeds;
the trick is pinning down what those are—

not a problem for her, if this man succeeds.
And who am I to hope that she'll rebel?
Surely, there are far worse childhoods

than running on the stairway of a *shul*
catching bits of language such as this.
Perhaps she'll listen to it. Who can tell?

Don't mistake me. I'm not envious
but it would be dishonest to pretend
that I don't notice the elaborate grace

available only to the hidebound.
It's an all-or-nothing business, piety,
not just inordinately disciplined,

but requiring, above all else, humility,
which is finally the thing that counts me out.
But for an instant, anyway, it seems a pity.

On the other hand, what do I know about
the thoughts beneath these wigs and huge black hats?
Maybe half these people are steeped in doubt

and the other half are flagrant hypocrites:
horribly vain, petty, deceitful, cruel,
their prayers a variation on the stylized florets

that cover every surface of their *shul*,
just one more exaggerated fashion,
equally rigid and fanatical

and, perhaps, equally devoid of passion.
Maybe this momentary sense of grace
is a function of my own imagination

and the ludicrous flamboyance of this place.
And even if the Torah was superbly read,
I have no right to this ridiculous

nostalgia for a thing I never had
and—had I survived it—would have hated.
Still, those verses do stay in my head

and others like them, equally exalted.
God's Torah is perfect, says the psalm
and who can argue with a giant-hearted,

if somewhat errant, poet king, whose realm
has just now entered its fourth millennium,
if a hundred-fifty poems is a realm.

Besides, I love the vastness of the claim
and—depending, of course, how you define *perfection*—
am inclined entirely to agree with him.

Call it sentiment; call it protection
against heartlessness, homelessness, the evil eye.
Maybe I'm just sick of indirection,

though, now, I can't even make my way
through the chanted text: haftarah, more melodic,
but completely unavailable to me.

You'd think I'd at least recognize the book.
(Did he just say Elisha? Maybe Kings?)
I should know what goes with the binding of Isaac,

but then I should know a lot of things,
which is why I can't renounce the people who know.
Look what care they take of my belongings,

when I, myself, have all but let them go.
They'll even keep safe for me my sabbath day
while I'm off ogling the Paolo Uccello

and pray the daily prayers I never pray.
I absolutely count on their intransigence;
I wouldn't want all of us to go astray.

You never know. One day, I might learn reverence
or simply need a perfect word to say
or even to overhear as some believer chants
before I continue on my way.

At the Wailing Wall

I figure I have to come here with my kids,
though I'm always ill at ease in holy places—
the wars, for one thing—and it's the substanceless
that sets me going: the holy words.
Though I do write a note—my girls' sound future
(there's an evil eye out there; you never know)—
and then pick up a broken-backed siddur,
the first of many motions to go through.
Let's get them over with. I hate this women's section
almost as much as that one full of men
wrapped in tallises, eyes closed, showing off.
But here I am, reciting the *Amida* anyway.
Surprising things can happen when you start to pray;
we'll see if any angels call my bluff.

Spring Sonnet, with My Sister's Favorite Bit of Deborah

The way I see it, every season comes through
with a blessing—winter: dazzle; summer: evening;
autumn: cold; and, this particular spring
it's got to be you, monotonous cuckoo
or whatever you are, blasting that major third
like a downbeat for the music of the spheres.
And who's to say it isn't, that the stars
and planets aren't guided by a bird?
Your voice certainly seems to carry far
enough, its two persistent notes so pure
they'll keep the air's orchestra in tune.
Who cares if they're the same again and again?
I'll stop waiting for that new, exquisite song.
I've got two notes; *even I will sing.*

Villanelle

This chill in spring—my subtle ally—
The elements all blossoming at once—
New snow on the mountains, lupines in the valley,

Like a rare conjunction of planets, ideally
Stationed for a long spell of disturbance.
This chill in spring—my subtle ally—

Will not suffer ice to let go easily
And I envy its immaculate resistance.
New snow on the mountains, lupines in the valley.

Will the air give lessons? See how coolly
It ambushes the lilacs' shrill abundance,
This chill in spring—my subtle ally.

But how has it managed so uncannily
To find me out? I burned the evidence.
And what about snow, lupines, mountains, valley?

The whole earth is unreconciled, unruly.
I'm just one tiny dissonance.
This subtle spring, this chilling ally.
New snow on the mountains, lupines in the valley.

Saskatchewan Sonnets

I.

Why so prostrate, prairies? What do you see?
and to whom are you offering this incense?
It can't be for that puny scrap of tree,
though it *does* cut quite a figure from this distance.
So, I suppose, from where *it* stands, do I.
Is that why I love it here, because I'm tall
for once? My only competition is the sky
and even that is much lower than usual.
What a boon to this exhausted heaven:
someplace it can finally lie down
and in green pastures, just like the psalm!
Is that rain or is its cup just running over?
But David never mentioned this perfume.
Who needs frankincense where there's sweet clover?

II.

What's going on down there? A bacchanal?
It's like an opium den for insects, this sweet clover.
Do you think they'll reel around like this forever
or get to sleep it off after a while?
Who knew a bee could function upside down?
That a tipsy, autodidact butterfly
could deduce the secret of perpetual motion
(some electron must have given it away)
and spread the hectic knowledge with her wings.
Now there's a tactic I could sorely use,
though I'd settle for the musical notation
of this buzzing's asymmetric harmonies
(unless I'm also having a hallucination?),
how this chaos, from my feet forward, sings.

III.

Maybe I'll learn something from these prairies:
so determined to extend themselves
they can't take time from rolling up their sleeves
to bother with the usual trappings of grandeur
(not—look around—that they're in any danger).
They have mouths to feed, they're getting old
and a load of equally persistent worries:
this perfect growing weather; will it hold?
But, as if against their will, the grandeur's happened.
Watch the staggered curtsy of that barley in the field,
how a single breeze unlocks its treasuries.
Low to the ground or not, these no-nonsense prairies
are still comprised of filaments of gold
and nothing earthly moves like gold in wind.

IV.

Look how well this landscape does without us:
no middle distance, just earth and sky . . .
as if to make completely unambiguous
that there isn't room for us. We're temporary.
Astonishingly blunt, if nothing new;
we're lucky to be tolerated at all.
But how long can such a pinched good will—
in this expanse of harshness—continue?
Remember the enormous cache of dinosaur bones
unearthed nearby; that tyrannosaurus
had no option but to disappear.
Such bullies, these prairies, going on forever—
or is this their one lesson in endurance:
Just keep your heads down. Follow us.

Again, at San Giorgio degli Schiavoni

You'd think I'd move on to something else
or at least grow accustomed to the shock.
But what can I tell you? It still dazzles,

still sends my clumsy eyes into a panic,
not just to catch it all before it fades,
but to memorize each item as a keepsake.

(Like I need more dragons' eyes and gold brocades.)
But it's not a dream. Or not mine anyway.
It won't dissolve it all; look how it spreads

across the walls for anyone to see.
A room. Four painted walls. It's really there
and kind enough to do my dreaming for me

if I would let it, if I could stand here
awash in all this lush, unsorted clutter,
not caring if a single thing comes clear.

Maybe a flash or two of unclaimed glitter
would even take a chance and land on me.
Why not let it? What does it matter

whether that's a dragon or a tree,
a saint or monster, a boat or shoe?
Why am I so frantic to supply

an accurate account, complete with follow-through?
Why do I always have to get my bearings?
Then again, who is this guy Carpaccio

that I should lose myself in his meanderings?
Does he get lost in mine? What's he to me?
I doubt he had to hear some poet's murmurings

before he placed that pheasant near that tree.
Ah, but I'm wrong again. Look! There I am!
Unobtrusive, in the far-left corner. See?

At the painting's margins: there are three of them:
inflating their already puffed-out cheeks
to give more color to the bright encomium

waiting in their trumpets' upraised necks.
Can you see the likeness? *I'm* always praising things;
it's my definition of poetics.

I learned it from my favorite ancient king's
favorite pastime (aside from women);
he preferred an instrument of ten strings

but, in a pinch, was always quick to summon
a couple of trumpet blasts to crank things up.
That's why I see these three men as an omen.

I admit, my comparison's a little bankrupt;
I haven't got a trumpet, only this
and I'm not even sure I'm that adept.

But look at my three guys: hellbent, tenacious;
maybe what I mean is how we've yearned,
my trumpeters and I, inconspicuous

in a stunning cityscape's congested background.
And they're disgusted with their tone; it's much too shrill,
just as Carpaccio, who longed to make a sound,

found his silent brushes unacceptable.
Still, it's not as if I have a trumpet.
I'm more like that lady at her window still

eyeing George parading down the street.
She probably doesn't see the real thing either.
That's what this is, by the way, did I tell you that?

Carpaccio's St. George—though I've seen other
such trumpeters in paintings from that era.
I'm always so delirious to find them there.

I envy their oblivious bravura,
the way they struggle toward that perfect fanfare:
Who cares if anyone's listening? Abracadabra.

Let's just fill our cheeks with still more air.
All this vast intensity is theirs.
George slays his dragon with far less ardor,

his bride almost lethargic through her tears,
but how my virtuosos' faces resonate
as muses cram cadenzas in their ears.

Come on, guys. You can play them. Concentrate.
Just picture one pure note and watch it rise
up through your trumpet's bell. Now let it out.

Don't stop while I readjust my eyes.
You can't fool me, Carpaccio; that's your self-portrait,
clamoring for one last blast of praise.

IV

Slim Fantasia on a Few Words from Hosea

Take words with you and return to God . . .
—Hosea 14:3

I.

Poor Hosea, who
can stomach him?—
marrying that
harlot, leaving
her to languish
in the desert,
giving his own kids
those vile names.
Not to mention
speeches full of
graphic retribution.
Probably the people—
if they ever gathered
in the first place—
after a phrase or two
just walked away.
Me? I can't even
read him on an ideal
afternoon at the perfect
distance of a holy
language. But it
turns out I'm the one
he's talking to: hey,
big-mouth poet,
lifting the gem-
stones from the Bible:
*take words with you
and return to God.*

II.

I love the way
he doesn't say
which ones.
I'm tempted to
bring along the
entire dictionary;
that way, God can
choose whatever words
He likes. But what
if He starts ripping
out whole pages,
declaring everything
on them and their
synonyms off-limits,
says: okay, I'll take
praise, Torah, God.
You can find your
own words; leave Me
out of this. But
here's a tip: you're
focused on the wrong
half of the quotation.
The important section
is *return to God.*

III.

By which He'd
have a point,
but what if He
doesn't tell me
how to get there?
Where did I think
I was heading
with my OED?

The Holy Temple's
been destroyed.
And in its place
—according to
the radio this
very morning—
they've got live
bullets and a
vindictive crowd
shouting something
in Arabic I can't
make out, but it isn't
*take words with you
and return to God.*

IV.

It's not as if—by
the way—I have
any kind of handle
on what is meant
here by the word
return. When,
exactly, was I
ever with Him?
The closest I've
come, if I've
been in the vicinity
at all, has only
ever been a matter
of words: the kind
Hosea's after,
interchangeable
with beaten gold,
that show up in
the lining of the
holy of holies

I didn't know
was lodged
inside my brain. . . .

V.

Maybe it's like
an algebraical
equation, in which
the word *and*
stands in for *equals*
until *take words*
with you means
return to God.

VI.

Or maybe I was
wrong about
that crowd;
Hosea's words
were uttered, but
with a different
intonation; it's an
imperative to die:
return to God.
And *take words*
with you is the
stone-thrower's
signal that he's
throwing stones
because he's tired
of words and more
words, especially
the ones delivered
by an inaudible

Landlord, whose
ancient promises
have now expired.

VII.

But shouldn't I
describe this day,
another perfect one?
The sky, as usual,
uninterrupted . . .
only at its edge,
a strip of cloud,
the torn-off fragment
of a holy page
reading: *take*
words with you
and return to God.

VIII.

I'd love to take
dictation on a
cloud; I'd pluck
a feather from a
passing cormorant
and moisten it with
remnants from a
seven-sided snow-
flake, sequestered
in an overly warm
fog. At least I think
it might make an
imprint on a cloud.
Then, if I found a
way to fold it up,

I'd take it with me
and return to God.

IX.

Or maybe I'd be
returning to Hosea,
or not Hosea, but
the scalding place
I suspect Hosea's
words have been
or not—let's be
realistic—the very
place; I'd settle for
their general direction. . . .

X.

Of course, needless
to say, I'd lose
sight of them.
Even my one cloud
has disappeared.
Heaven's rejoicing,
it can finally get
back on schedule
delivering its daily
empty aerogram.
And I, like a fool,
will stand here,
squinting at the sun,
reading the entire
text aloud. Don't
tell me it's empty.
I'll take any inter-
ruption, anything

the sky will dare
to hold, anything
but Hosea and his
crackpot exhortation:
*Take words with you
and return to God.*

Snorkeling at Coral Beach/ Fish in the Torah

We don't find the names of fish anywhere in the Torah.

—S.Y. Agnon, *Only Yesterday*

Maybe God didn't want to steal Adam's thunder.
Though why Anyone would stick by that inveterate nebbish
is beyond me: I bet he's still under
that same fig tree, still stuck at antelope
(Gnu? Oryx? Addax? Nilgai? Springbok?).
Too bad he never got to see a map:
with three seas (well, two alive) and one huge lake,
he might have branched out and named a fish.

I can see why God might not bother to mention lemurs,
armadillos, yaks, iguanas, polar bears
(though it must at least have crossed His mind
to use a few as backup from the whirlwind)—
but never to identify one fish?
Not that the generic isn't useful
(Jonah's whale is just *big fish*—*dag gadol*)
but I thought God's great talent was to distinguish

among specifics. And it's real-live spectacle,
this Red Sea. Signs and wonders in continuation.
God could have saved a lot of aggravation.
Admittedly, ancient Israel had no snorkel,
but compared to ten plagues, what's an aquarium?
Besides, look at Mark Spitz—a Jew can swim.
My four-year-old saw the colors from the shore;
how could a whole people miss that lavender,

that orange, yellow, mauve, electric blue?
And what about the time we walked right through,
an enormous wall of water on either side?
Where were the lionfish, angelfish, clownfish,

parrotfish, needlefish, Picassofish?
Some prophet could have used the new material.
Who knows? It might at last explain Ezekiel:
and the waters *opened and I saw visions of God:*

Think about it. It's right up his alley:
hordes of floating angels, eagles, lions,
their vast assortment of translucent fins,
his triple sets of incandescent wings.
Remember *the noise of many waters?* It really
happened! It was the Red Sea, not the Chebar River;
I'm the first to blow Ezekiel's cover!
And for years, I've accused him of seeing things,

indulging himself in psilocybin mushrooms
or—at the very least—the local hashish.
But the only psychedelics were the *fish,*
which turn out to be the inverse of hallucinogens
since they're *real*, and you *don't* believe your eyes.
The Red Sea's the sapphire inner sanctum,
white coral reefs, the throngs of rising bones.
Where could you find a more affecting sacrifice

than the way this utterly bereft horizon
relinquishes its armory of colors:
pleading with the sea to pull them under
and shield them from a homicidal sun?
The waves are flabbergasted, it's no wonder
they'll take any excuse to clap their hands.
They want to see what their diligent jewelers
have left around their fingers this time: bands

of emerald, sapphire, ruby, beaten gold.
Who begrudges them their unchecked noise?
They're only trying to clue us in
to God's amazing ongoing balancing act:
His earth, it turns out—like His Torah—is perfect!
A streak of gorgeousness in every portion,

if, at times, hermetically concealed.
There must be hosts of things that aren't known to us:

ruby, emerald, sapphire, beaten gold.
At least, at the Red Sea, you can use a camera.
So why would I want its beauties in the Torah
where only the invisible is revealed?
As if God would waste His lyric impulse
on the obvious. Who can't see Eilat?
So He created gorgeous fish. What else
is new? And if I'm really so desperate

to know every outlandish species' name,
I can use my free chart from the aquarium.
The Torah is not a treatise on zoology;
God is far more subtle with His words.
And I also owe Ezekiel an apology:
that *waters* bit was a cheap contrivance;
what opened up before him was the *heavens*.
That's why the Torah names so many birds.

Hearing News from the Temple Mount in Salt Lake City

You know that conversation
in the elevator in the Catskills:
how one woman says, *Oy,*
the food here is so terrible
and the other *and the portions*
are so small? It's a variant
on Jacob's line to Pharaoh
when he gets to Egypt—*few*
and evil have been the days
of my life. Naturally, he's our
chosen namesake: this Israel
the Torah keeps forgetting and
calling Jacob, as if it doesn't
trust his cleaned-up name.

Obviously he's the perfect
guy for us—we're always
willing to take something
over nothing—hence
our lunatic attachment
to that miserable pinpoint
in the desert, where now,
whether it's Ishmael
or Isaac on the altar,
there's an earsplitting
crowd working to drown
out every angel until
Abraham fulfills his sacrifice.

It's none of my diaspora-
befuddled business, but
I'm not in the mood

to celebrate. Call me
thin-skinned, but I can't
get used to the idea that
all these hordes of people
wish me dead. You have
to remember: I'm Jacob's
offspring; I want as many
evil days as I can lay my
hands on. Thank God
I live in Salt Lake City. Who's
going to come looking for me
here? In this calm Zion,
where a bunch of blonde
meshugeners think *they're*
the chosen people of God.
Good luck to them is all
I have to say; let them
get the joy from it that I do.

Soreq

My first thought is:
it comes as recompense
for the acres of austerity
above it, as if even
the most unlikely
stretch of harshness
has its necessary
ration of flamboyance.

But is there such a thing
as recompense? And do
I really want to imagine
every empty tract of land
with its own inflexible
extravaganza, its complicated

beauty happening without
us—a conspiracy of
chalk, lime, water, eons
and nothing external
whatsoever, not even,
if I'm not mistaken, air?

I'm doing damage just
by being here; they only
know about this place by
accident: a quarry blast
some twenty years ago:
the solid rock not solid
rock at all, but a hollow
overrun with grotesque
frippery: sturdy ghosts
of everything that grows

or maybe the forgotten
death mask of Babylon's
hanging gardens, turned
asylum for a banished
gang of idols. For all
I know, they're still
awaiting worshippers
—what's another
twenty billion years?
Meanwhile, they're right
beneath the very outskirts
earmarked for a din
of exultation. Jeremiah
was too smart to give
a time frame, but I'd say
it's profoundly overdue.
Still, at this point, I'm
willing to settle for a long,
wide-open spell of silence

or even a dependable
and harmless noise:
the steady dripping
from the ceiling of
this cave, aching to
contribute (it will
take a hundred
years) its new half-
centimeter to some
lucky stalactite. How
I envy its underground
oblivion . . . its constant,
if somewhat dim-
witted, progress.

These very stalag-
mites and stalactites
may well have been
the prophet's target

audience: *earth,*
earth, earth, hear
the word of the Lord

Perhaps, you need
duration to under-
stand him. Though it
couldn't hurt to tighten
up my lackadaisical
Hebrew. I'm not even
sure I got this tour guide
right: *did* he say chalk,
lime, a hundred years?

And did Jeremiah
really say: *Again*
there will be heard
in this place
you call desolate. . .
in the cities of Judah
and the outskirts
of Jerusalem . . .
a voice of joy
a voice of gladness,
a voice of a bridegroom
a voice of a bride?

What if this dripping
is the voice of gladness . . .
stalagmite and stalactite:
the groom and bride?
Suppose this prophecy
was long ago fulfilled,
but just had nothing
whatsoever to do with us.

Maybe it's not this
desolate place, but
our own insignificance

we're fighting about.
Adam and Eve just
didn't have the stamina.
(Clearly, Eden was under-
ground.) Or perhaps they
simply never understood
their brand-new habitat's
unnerving tempo. Who
can blame them if they
wanted to exceed

five centimeters in a
thousand years? I know
I'd overtake them if I
could. But every day
I'm a bit less clear
on precisely what
is evil, what is good.

The Hoopoe's Crown

I suppose it's something I should embrace:
how a one-time sighting of a feathered crown—
before it's even recorded—becomes a treatise

on suffering and human limitation.
I couldn't remember one particular
of the legend of the hoopoe and King Solomon

only (from the picture) the fiery color,
how the fanned-out feathers *do* contrive a crown.
It was always my weakness—the spectacular—

I'd never have made the same request as Solomon.
For one thing, his judgments leave me cold;
I don't believe the world contains a woman—

real mother or not—who would have settled
for half the body of a divided infant,
or fall for such a threat: a child killed?

If this is wisdom's highest achievement,
it has to be a fairly hollow thing.
And then, when you consider its denouement:

how the man we acknowledge as our wisest king
finished up his life worshipping idols.
But I'm ahead of myself; I was telling

or planning to tell some old Near Eastern riddles,
like how the hoopoe got his feathered crown.
Solomon *is* involved; it's he who straddles

an earlier riddle's eagle, on a mission
to explore the farthest reaches of his kingdom.
But he's failed to factor in the pounding sun

(apparently, the refinements of his wisdom
don't extend themselves to head coverings).
The tale: a flock of hoopoes flies straight over him

and makes a canopy of outspread wings,
shading him for his entire expedition.
In my version, each pair of hoopoes sings

an ornate variation on a two-part canon
(from these, the Song of Songs will be compiled)
alternating wingbeats so no drop of sun

can penetrate the airy, makeshift shield.
A crown is the hoopoe's chosen reward,
and, against all warnings, he wants it gold.

Needless to say, he's mercilessly snared
for the easy, precious bounty on his head
until, his numbers dwindling, the humbled bird

accepts a crown of feathers in its stead,
which is where I begin to take an interest:
potential evidence, or, at least, a lead

in my increasingly maniacal quest
for even an inkling of divine collusion
in the bauble, the ornament, the *beau geste*—

something unaccounted for by evolution.
And don't try to tell me that the frivolous,
by definition, needs no justification.

I'm finding that you can't stave off unhappiness
by obsessive fussing over a hoopoe's crown;
probably, it's just too late for this.

I should have dashed it off that afternoon
still reeling from the heady dose of grace:
a garden overlooking the Mediterranean

my family pretending to be as rapturous
as I was when a pair of orange wings
landed right beside us on the grass.

Then, I might have done without the meanings,
but I thought I'd use that hoopoe as an overture:
I'd find the forgotten folktale, reread Kings—

crazy—when I'd just witnessed a creature
so much like a product of sheer artifice
I had to reconceive my notion of nature,

especially in that rumor-driven place
(this was the land of Israel, just north of Akko)
and, clearly, Whoever had made this bird for us

was a thorough devotee of pure rococo.
That should have been the revelation.
Why assume that something must have gone askew

if a bird wears an orange-feathered crown?
Imbibe some cockamamie explanation
about a king on an eagle in the baking sun?

Why not revel in ornamentation?
Clearly—look at the Temple—that's what Solomon did
for all his genius at deliberation,

and his was a wisdom straight from God,
who, with His typical lack of foresight,
threw in every other prize he had

until He'd made His own will obsolete:
immense riches, lands, power, women.
But if you ask me, Solomon was no more astute

than a bird tempting hunters with a crown.
Wasn't each gold cherub on the gold facade
of his over-the-top temple an invitation

to local thugs to plunder and maraud?
And isn't it, itself, a kind of idolatry—
all that gold, ivory, cedar, acacia wood—

or, at the very least, the height of folly?
The heaven's my throne, the earth's my footstool
(this is God talking) *what house can you build Me?*

I'm sorry. But Solomon's a fool.
Unless—he *was* wise, wasn't he?—he always knew
that all that admittedly absurd detail

was, frankly, the best that he could do.
Poor guy. It was faith he should have asked for;
think of the heartache of going through

that ridiculous charade, to manufacture
a vast and necessarily empty place.
Not that he thought extravagant expenditure

would replace faith—he wasn't fatuous—
but maybe he allowed himself the sneaking hope
that all that complicated enterprise

would, in its intensity, catch him up
and he'd find himself, in all its glare, believing.
Isn't that what I think . . . when I take up

some crazy subject . . . and try to make it sing?
I keep thinking, this time, I'll get it all:
not just the hoopoe's crown, the orange wing,

that headcase Solomon, the Hebrew Bible,
but my own lostness, without explaining
even a single miserable detail.

But I'll also forget some vital covering,
and what flock of birds would bail me out?
Believe me, I'll take sparrows, starlings, anything

or better still—but here I'm pushing it;
since it's not as if I have a crown to give—
I'd trade the whole flock for even brief delight

on my husband's face—I won't say love,
since his is so entwined with bitterness,
and, at best, completely uncommunicative,

except that day, with the hoopoe on the grass
when he seemed to take such pleasure in my pleasure
along with our three daughters—was it avarice

on my part? Should a wife and mother
let her family indulge her in that way?
He even managed to get a picture

of my hoopoe just before he flew away,
perhaps to make some king another canopy?
It's on a diskette somewhere, stashed away.

Who knows? Maybe, if I asked him for a copy,
he'd actually be glad to print one out.
He'd be happy for a minute. I'd be happy.

But I don't believe it; in fact, I doubt
he wants anything more than to be left alone.
So what choice do I have? I'm about

to do precisely that, for the duration,
when for years, I regretted that a mere lifetime
was all we'd have. I'm overthrown,

though I was full of love and faith; I still am
but it doesn't look like either one can save me.
Clearly, the thing I lack is wisdom,

not to mention a feathery canopy
to shield me from a brutal, brutal sun.
I suppose I, too, am just too greedy,

like that colossal fuck-up, Solomon
and his vainglorious bird. My loving family
has been—a bit too much—my golden crown

and it was spectacular, if only briefly.
No feathers to replace it, only pain,
which I, like an idiot, thought poetry

might be able to help me undermine.
No luck. But I have learned something;
it's a bankrupt business, ornamentation,

idolatrous, at worst; at best, an aching
absence of whatever it is that matters.
A little wisdom is a relentless thing;

everywhere I look, something shatters.
And as for that protective flock of stunning birds,
I don't envy Solomon when it scatters.

God's Acrostic

What if the universe is God's acrostic?
He's sneaking bits of proverbs into seismic variations;
Abbreviating psalms in flecks of snow.
Try to read them, says a comet,

If you dare.
Fine print. What you've been waiting for.

Twisted in the DNA of marmosets:
Hermetic feedback to your tight-lipped prayer.
Examine indentations left by hailstones in the grass;

Unearth their parallel soliloquies;
Note, too, the shifting patterns of cuneiform
Initiating each communication.
Verify them. Don't take my word.
Eavesdrop on the planets in the outer spheres; they can
Reverse the letters' previous direction.
Silence, as you might imagine, has no bearing here.
Episodes of stillness—however brief—must be

Interpreted as unheard
Sounds,

Gaps that, with any luck, you'll fill in later—
Or so you tell yourself, acknowledging
Delusion's primal status in this enterprise.
Still, that's no reason to slow down.

Abandonments are howling out around you:
Cast off lamentations from the thwarted drops of rain
Reduced to vapor on their struggle down;
Observe, at the very least, their passing.
Sanctify them. Don't succumb

To anything less vivid than a spelled-out
Invitation to a not yet formulated nebula.
Calm yourself. Come quickly. Welcome home.

Acknowledgments

Antioch Review: "At the Wailing Wall" and "The Hoopoe's Crown";

Carolina Quarterly: "Soreq";

The Forward: "Hearing News from the Temple Mount in Salt Lake City";

Jubilat: "Judean Hills";

Listening with the Ear of the Heart: Writers at St. Peter's: "Saskatchewan Sonnets (I, III, IV)";

Michigan Quarterly Review: "Eccentric Fractals: Isaiah, Math, and Snow" and "Fata Morgana";

Paris Reivew: "Ri'e Yazmin";

Prairie Schooner: "Snorkeling at Coral Beach/ Fish in the Torah";

Princeton Library Chronicle: "Egrets in Be'er Sheva";

Radcliffe Quarterly: "Desert Postcards";

Slate: "Spring Sonnet, with My Sister's Favorite Bit of Deborah" and "God's Acrostic";

Southwest Review: "Autumn Psalm";

Tikkun: "Slim Fantasia on a Few Words from Hosea";

Western Humanities Review: "Again, at San Giorgio degli Schiavoni," "At the Art Nouveau Synagogue, Rue Pavée," "My Version: Medieval Acrostic," "The Stork in the Heaven," and "Villanelle."

The author gratefully acknowledges the help of the John Simon Guggenheim Foundation, the National Endowment for the Arts, the Hedgebrook Writers' Colony, the University of Utah Research Committee, the University of Utah Middle East Center and the Tanner Humanities Center of the University of Utah, the Saskatchewan Writers' Colony and The Eastend Saskatchewan Arts Council in writing many of the poems in this collection, and, as always, the invaluable help of Wayne Koestenbaum and Barry Weller.

About the Author

Jacqueline Osherow is the author of four previous books of poems: *Dead Men's Praise* (1999) and *With a Moon in Transit* (1996), both from Grove; and *Conversations with Survivors* (1993) and *Looking for Angels in New York* (1998), both from University of Georgia Press. Her work has appeared in many contemporary anthologies, including *The Best American Poetry*. She has been awarded fellowships from the Guggenheim Foundation, the National Endowment for the Arts, and the Ingram Merrill Foundation, and has received the Witter Bynner Prize from the American Academy and Institute of Arts and Letters, as well as a number of prizes from the Poetry Society of America. Osherow is Distinguished Professor of English at the University of Utah.

BOA Editions, Ltd., American Poets Continuum Series

Colophon

The Hoopoe's Crown, poems by Jacqueline Osherow,
was set in Caslon by Richard Foerster, York Beach, Maine.
The cover design is by Lisa Mauro;
the cover art, Ketubbah, Kouilvattam, 1909, is courtesy of
the Israel Museum, Jerusalem/Nahum Slapak.
Manufacturing was by McNaughton & Gunn, Lithographers,
Saline, Michigan.

The publication of this book was made possible, in part,
by the special support of the following individuals:

Alan & Nancy Cameros
Gwen & Gary Conners
Wyn Cooper
Suzanne & Peter Durant
Dr. Henry & Beverly French
Dane & Judy Gordon
Gerard & Suzanne Gouvernet
Donald & Marjorie Grinols
Kip & Deb Hale
Peter & Robin Hursh
Robert & Willy Hursh
Archie & Pat Kutz
Rosemary & Lewis Lloyd
James Longenbach
Boo Poulin
Deborah Ronnen
Paul & Andrea Rubery
Paul Tortorella
Pat & Michael Wilder